Octave

Scale Studies

for the Viola

Book One

by Cassia Harvey

CHP264

6403 N. 6th Street
Philadelphia, PA 19126
www.charveypublications.com

Octave Scale Studies for the Viola, Book One

1

Cassia Harvey

2

3

4

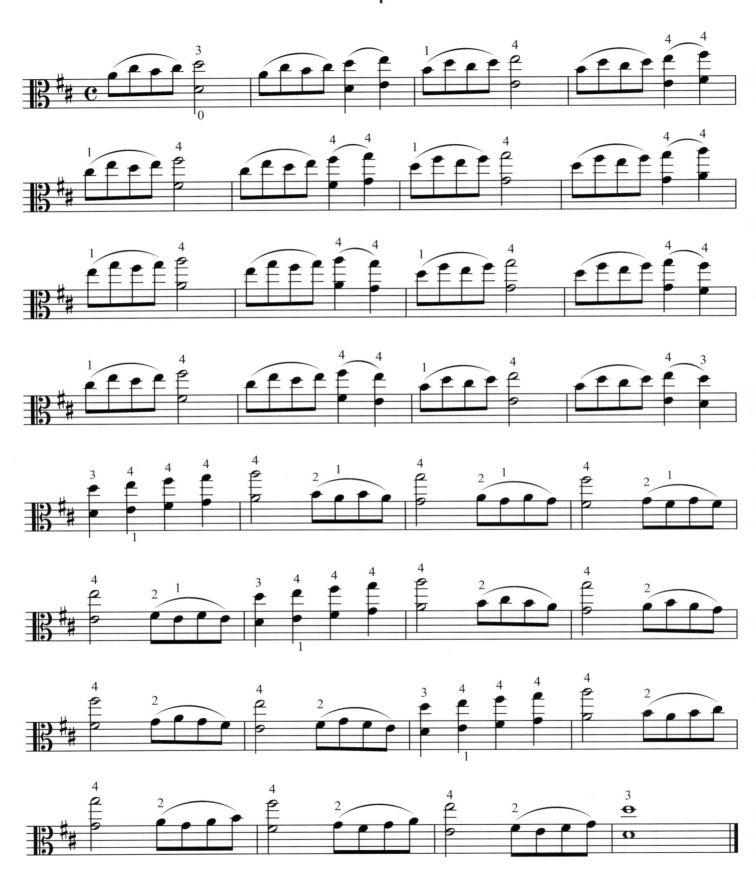

5

6

7

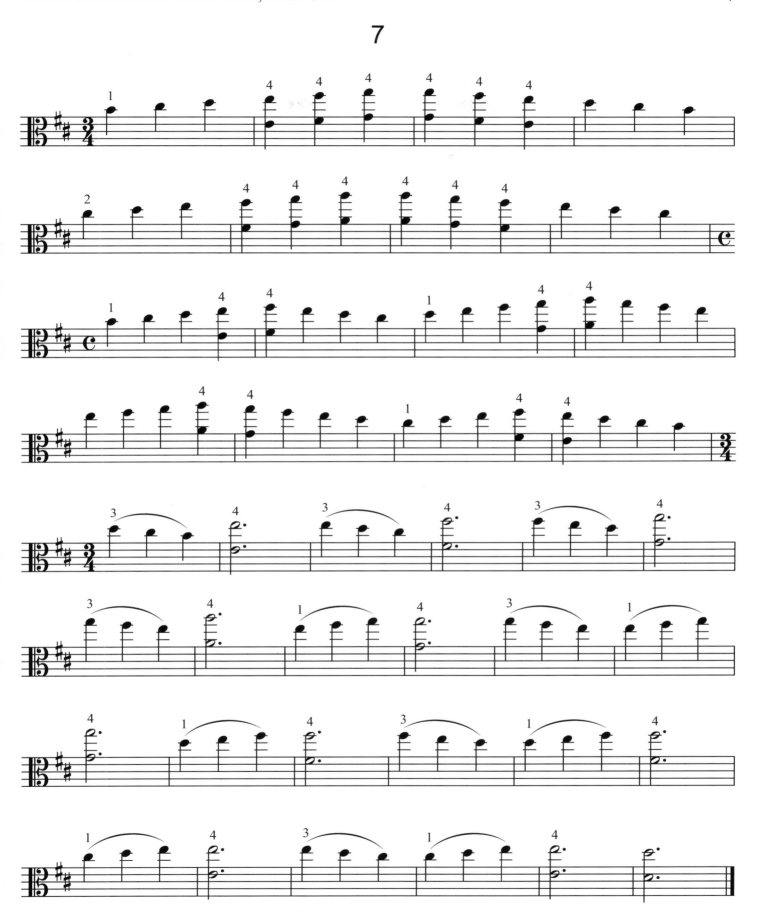

8

9

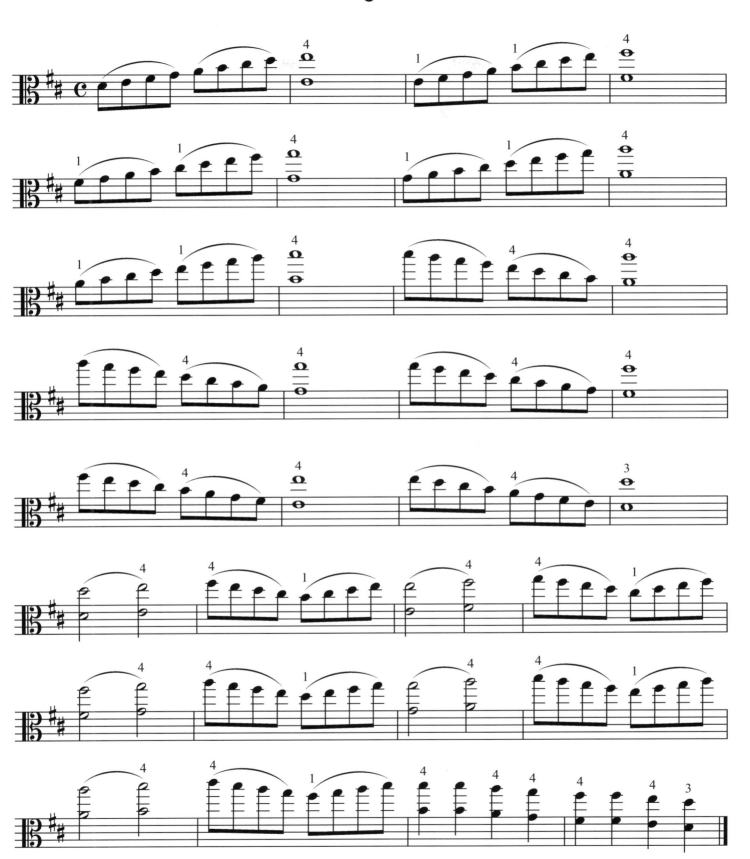

10

11

12

13

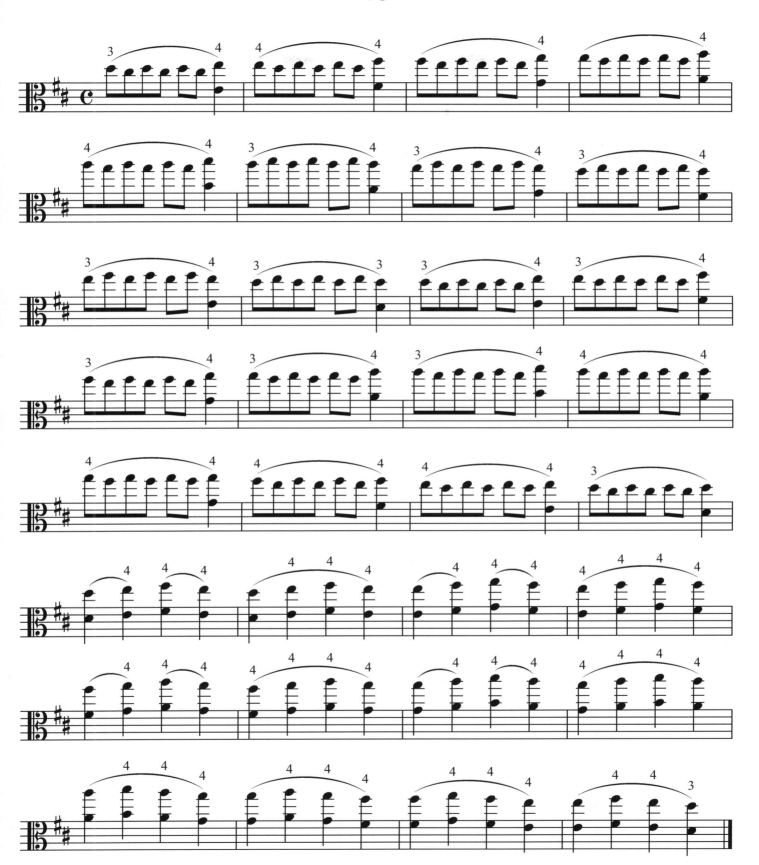

14

15

16

17

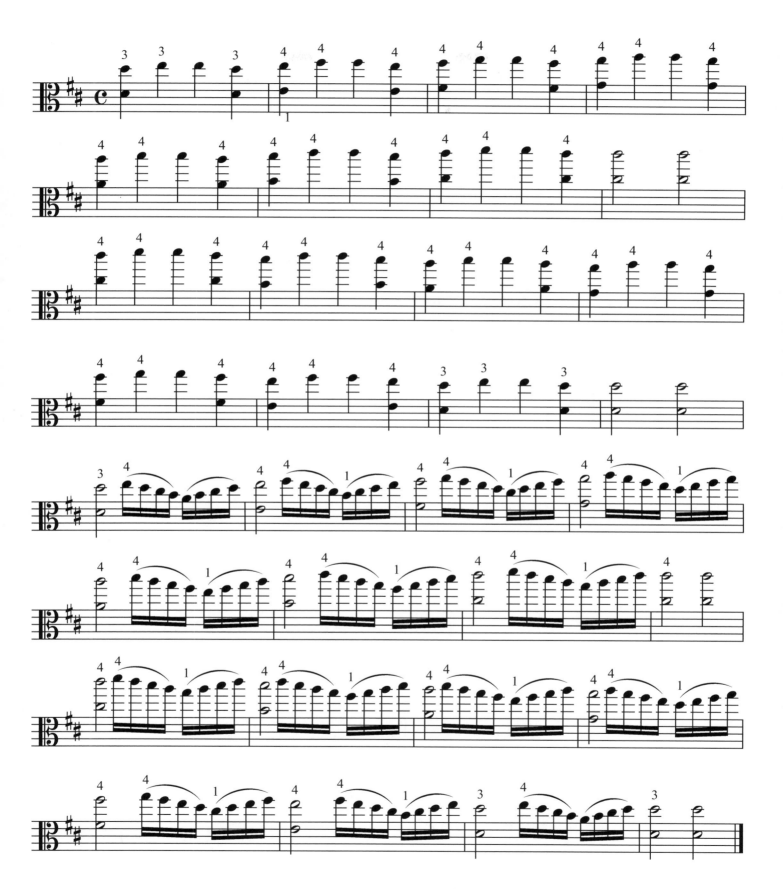

18

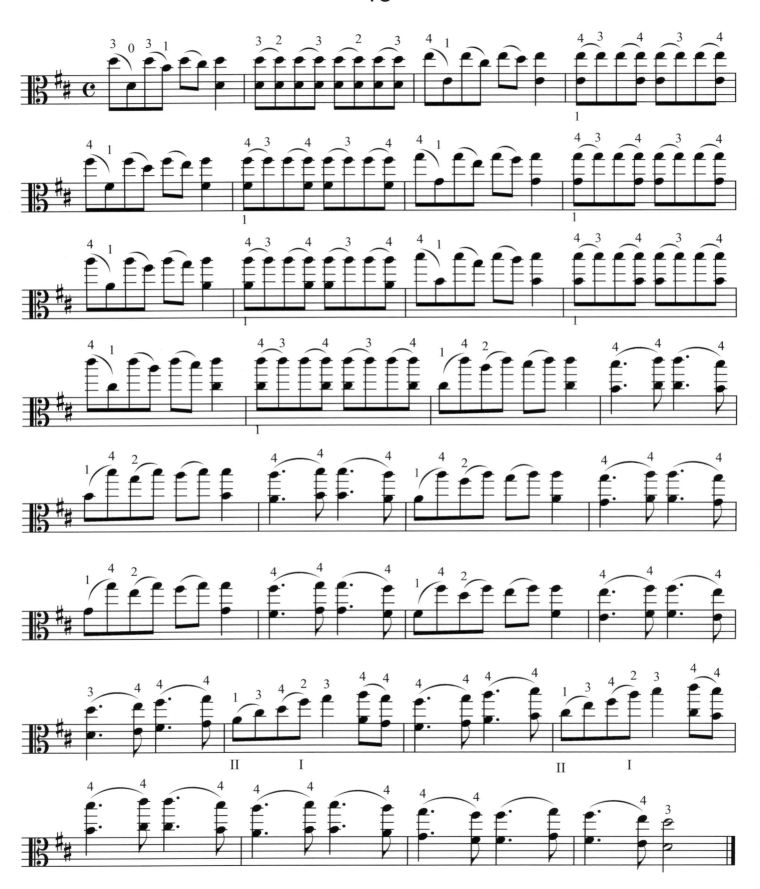

19

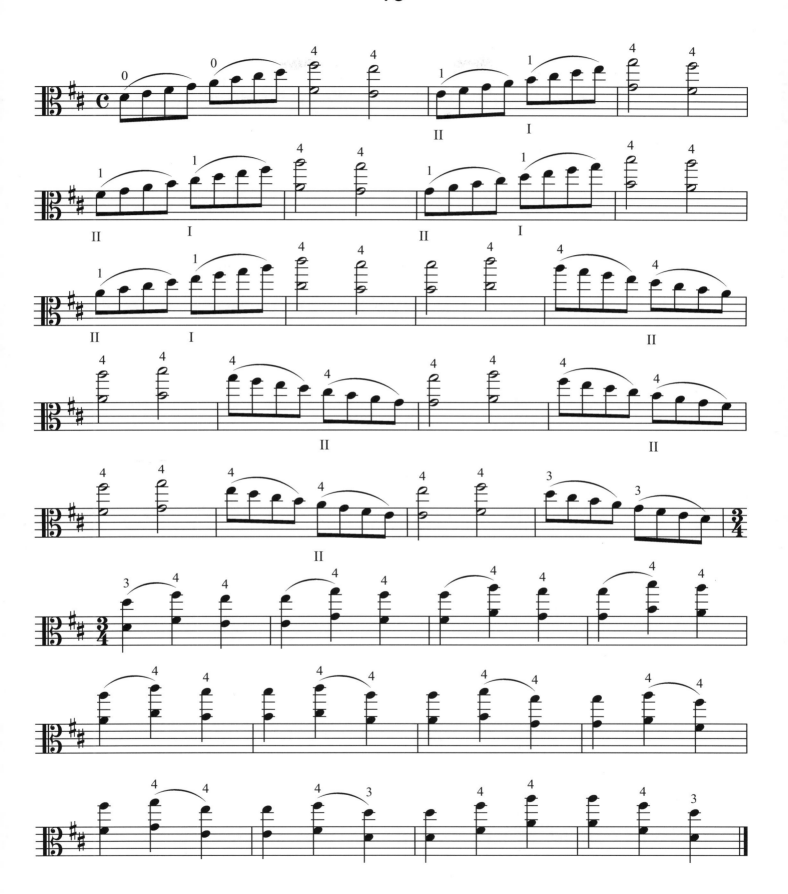

20

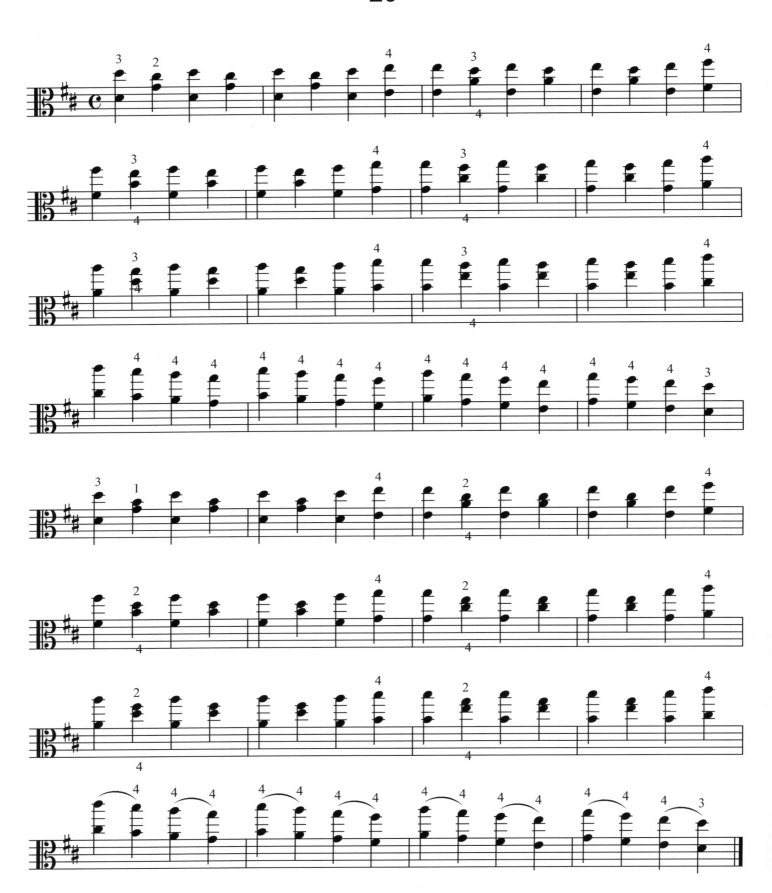

21

22

23

24

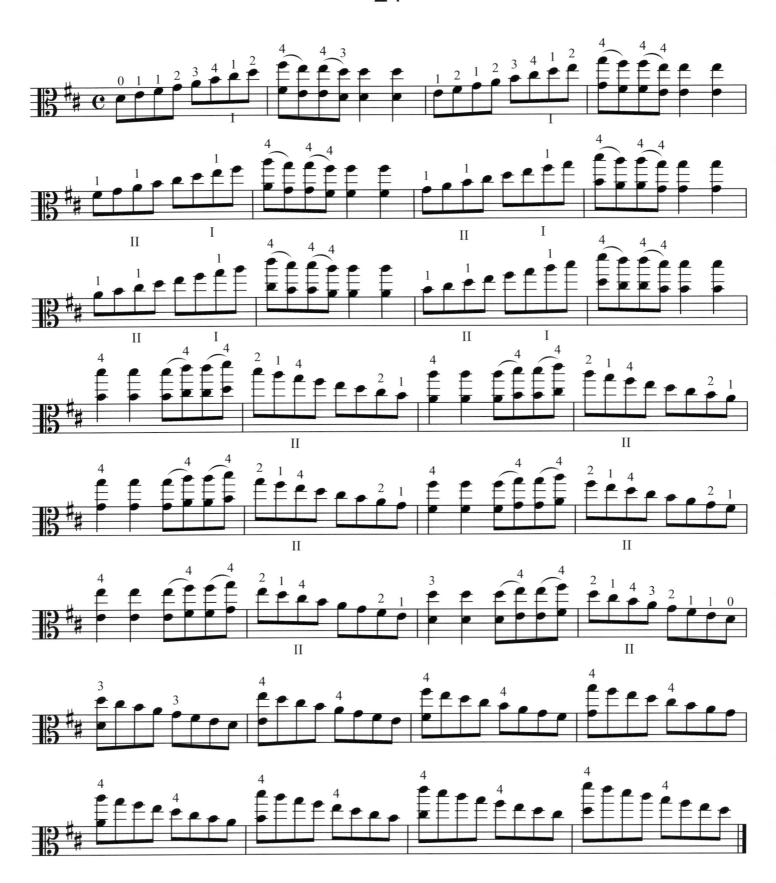

25

26

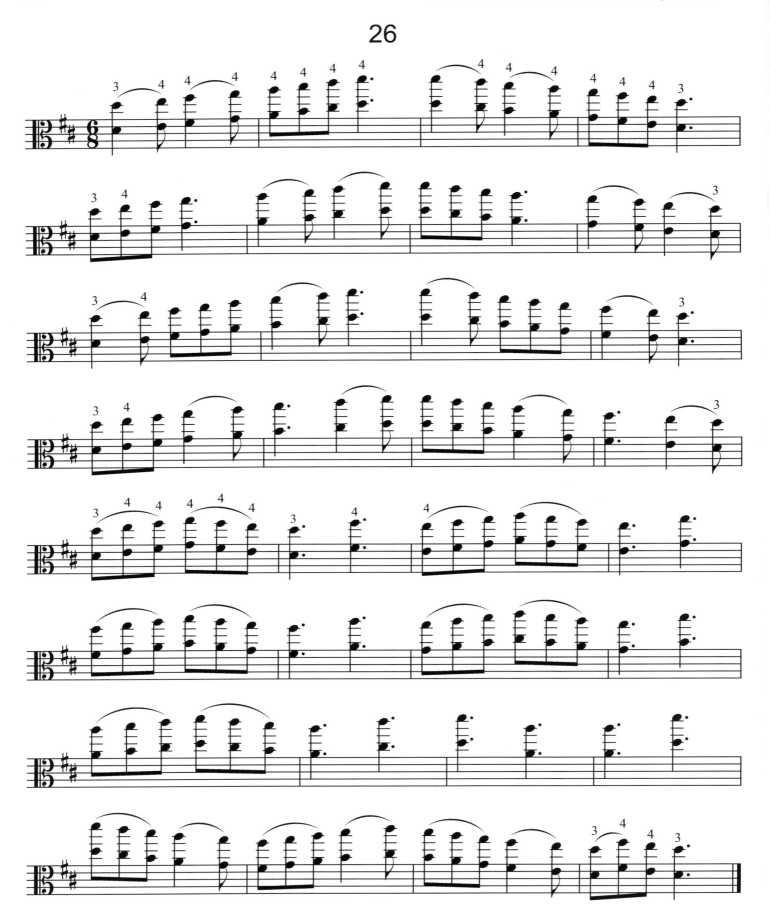

27

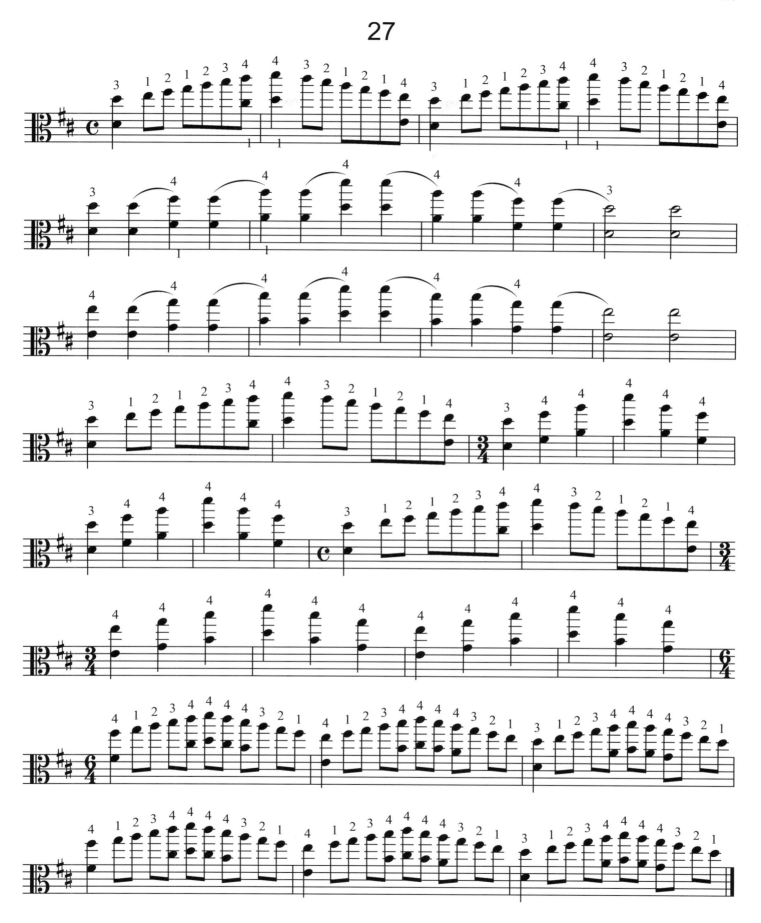

28

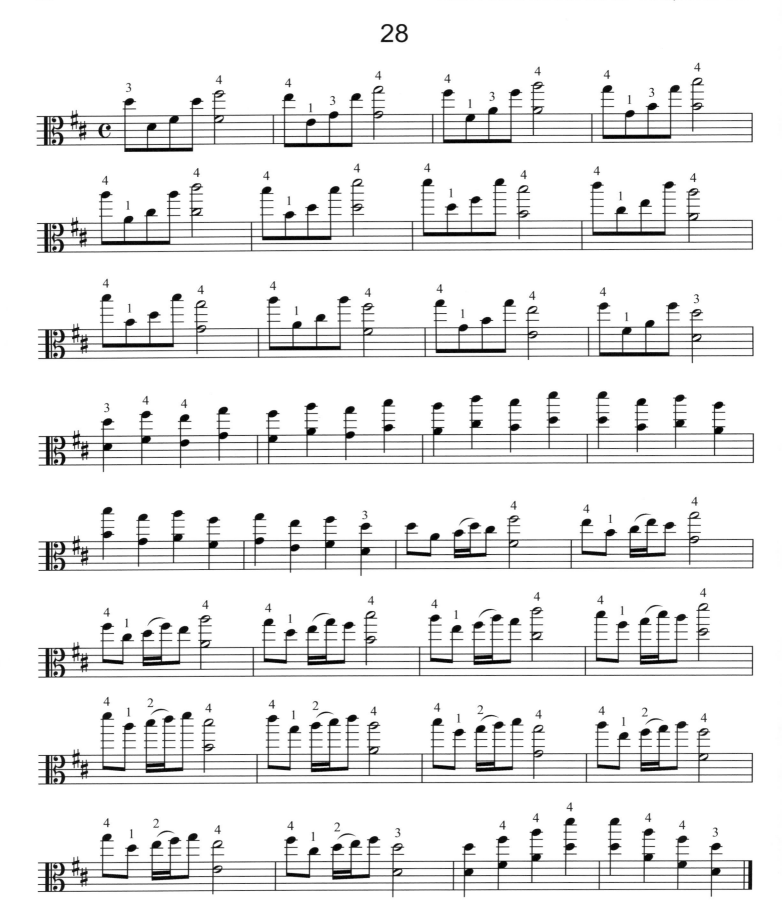

29

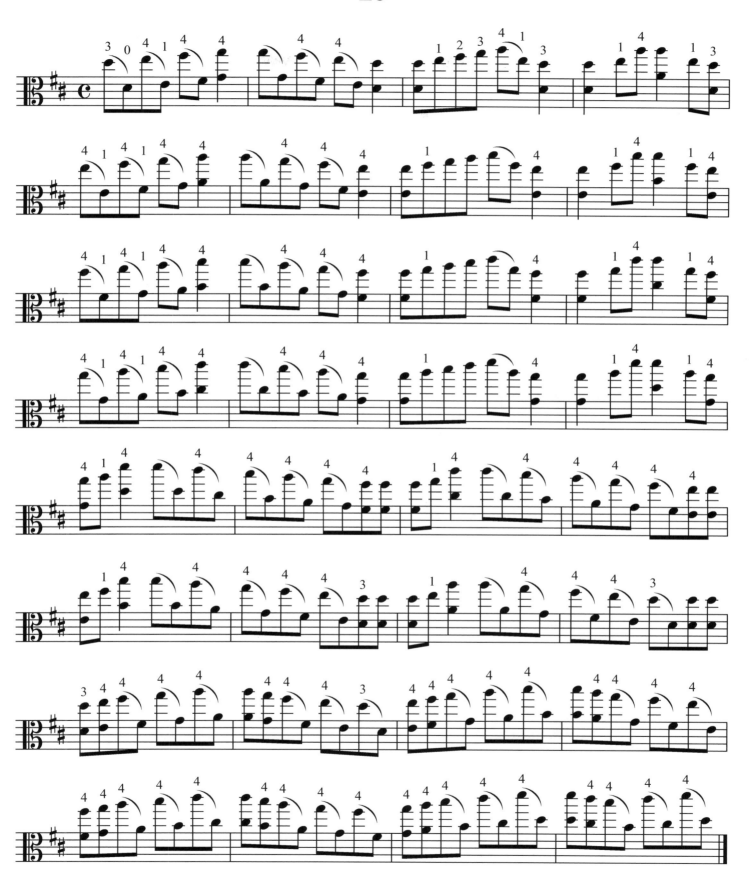

30

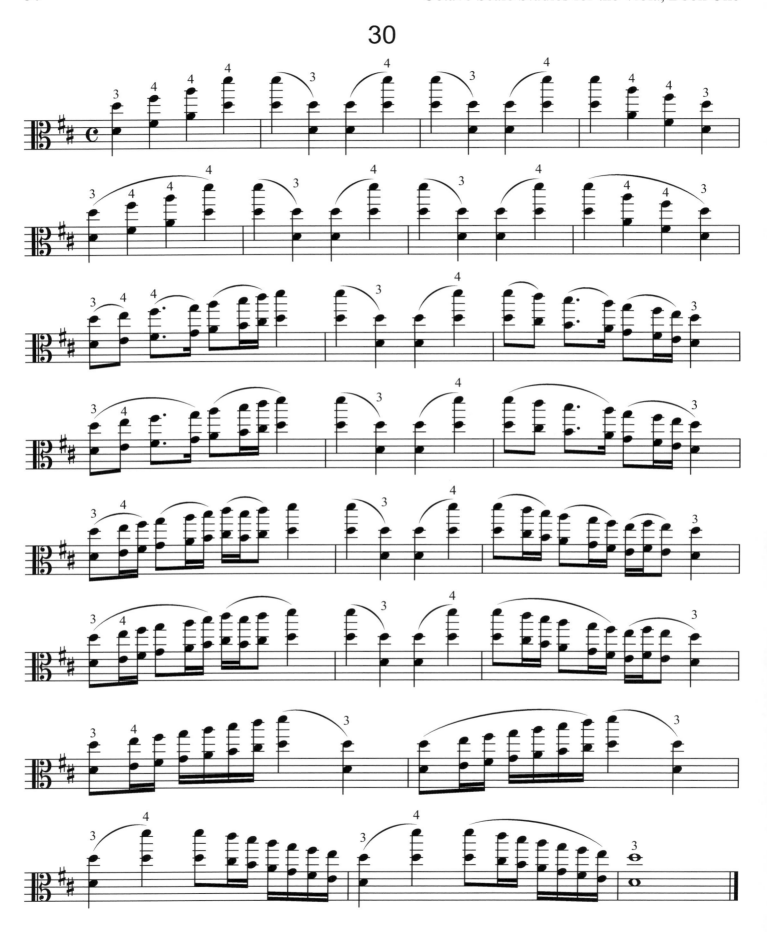

Fourth Position for the Viola

1

by Cassia Harvey

A. First Shifting on the A String

B. First Shifting on the D String

Made in the USA
Middletown, DE
31 January 2022

60038524R00020